CLOWNS

1. Scapino

PAUL HARRIS

CLOWNS

Seven pieces for flute and piano

(Grade II – III)

NOVELLO PUBLISHING LIMITED

8/9 Frith Street, London W1V 5TZ

Order No: NOV 120644

2. Pierrot

4

3. Pulcinella

4. Columbine

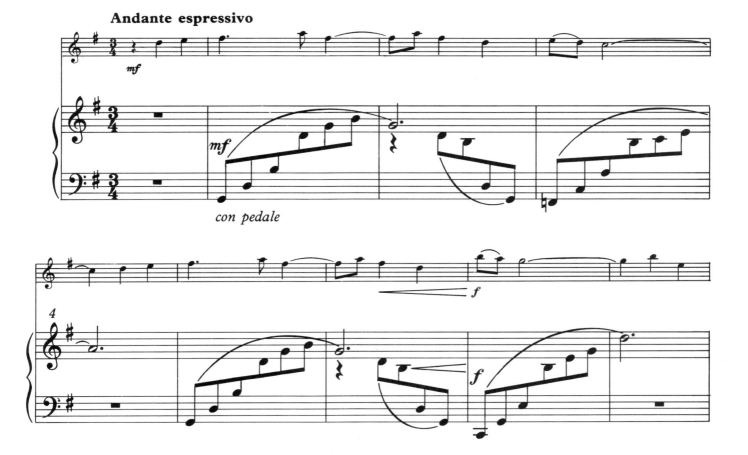

5. Harlequin

6. Pantalon

Moderato *(scherzando)*

7. Scaramouche

poco rall.　　　a tempo

Printed in Great Britain by Halstan & Co. Ltd., Amersham, Bucks.

TREVOR WYE

VIDEO

PLAY THE FLUTE
A beginner's guide

TUTORS

A BEGINNER'S BOOK FOR THE FLUTE
Part 1
Part 2
Piano Accompaniment

PRACTICE BOOKS FOR THE FLUTE
VOLUME 1 Tone (plus TONE CASSETTE available separately)
VOLUME 2 Technique
VOLUME 3 Articulation
VOLUME 4 Intonation and Vibrato
VOLUME 5 Breathing and Scales
VOLUME 6 Advanced Practice

A PICCOLO PRACTICE BOOK

PROPER FLUTE PLAYING

SOLO FLUTE

MUSIC FOR SOLO FLUTE

FLUTE & PIANO

A COUPERIN ALBUM
AN ELGAR FLUTE ALBUM
A FAURE FLUTE ALBUM
A RAMEAU ALBUM
A SATIE FLUTE ALBUM
A SCHUMANN FLUTE ALBUM
A VIVALDI ALBUM

A FIRST VERY EASY BAROQUE ALBUM
A SECOND VERY EASY BAROQUE ALBUM
A VERY EASY ROMANTIC ALBUM
A VERY EASY 20TH CENTURY ALBUM

A FIRST LATIN-AMERICAN FLUTE ALBUM
A SECOND LATIN-AMERICAN FLUTE ALBUM

MOZART FLUTE CONCERTO IN G K.313
MOZART FLUTE CONCERTO IN D K.314 AND ANDANTE IN C K.315

SCHUBERT THEME AND VARIATIONS D 935 No. 3

FLUTE ENSEMBLE

THREE BRILLIANT SHOWPIECES